Bob Hartman
More Bible Tales
The Unauthorized Version

Now for the other side of the story!

The Bible version of the Old and New Testament tales may be the official one. But there were plenty of characters on the sidelines who saw things from a different angle.

Packed full of humour, mischief, silliness, and fun: these unauthorized versions from master storyteller Bob Hartman get to the heart of the matter.

Bob Hartman knows how to captivate an audience, and regularly entertains children and adults around the world as a performance storyteller. He is perhaps best known for the widely acclaimed *Lion Storyteller Bible*. When he is not writing, Bob enjoys watching films, driving his cars, and entertaining his grandchildren.

Published by Lion Children's Books
an imprint of
Lion Hudson plc
Wilkinson House, Jordan Hill Road,
Oxford OX2 8DR, England
www.lionhudson.com/lionchildrens

ISBN 978 0 7459 6435 5
e-ISBN 978 0 7459 6806 3

First edition 2013

A catalogue record for this book is available from the British Library

Printed and bound in the UK, July 2013, LH26

Bob Hartman's More Bible Tales

THE UNAUTHORIZED VERSION

LION
CHILDREN'S

Contents

Introduction

You might have heard of a very famous English translation of the Bible called The Authorized Version. It's been around for just over 400 years. Well, I thought it might be fun to write an "Unauthorized" Version!

"Authorized" suggests "official" or "approved of". I figured that an unauthorized version, then, would come from someone who wasn't particularly official – from someone, maybe, that no one had even heard of. So I set about making up other voices to tell these familiar Bible stories. I wrote an Old Testament Version and New Testament Version, but there were voices from both testaments I still wanted to hear. So that's why there's a third volume, with voices like these:

- Noah's dog
- Judas's nephew
- a young man who couldn't keep his eyes open during one of Paul's sermons.

I tried to tell the stories in a way that would be true to the original, but also in a way that would bring out the humour in them.

I sort of doubt that anyone will be reading these in 400 years' time, but I hope that you enjoy them, and that you chuckle (at least a little). That will be approval enough for me.

Bob Hartman

Dog's Version

Noah and the Ark

Dog jumped up and down.

"Fox, Fox!" he woofed. "I need to talk to you. Right now."

Fox stuck a nose out of his hole.

"This doesn't have anything to do with your master's chickens, does it?" he asked, suspiciously.

"No, no! What chickens?" Dog woofed. "But it does have to do with my master."

"Never mind the chickens, then," Fox shrugged, sticking his head out as well. "So tell me about your master, if you must. Though why you insist on remaining in that ridiculous slave relationship escapes me."

"I know, I know!" Dog woofed. "But this time it might help. My master is building a boat. And I saved a seat, just for you!"

Fox pulled his shoulders out of the hole, and propped up his cheek on his paw. Then he chuckled.

"A boat, you say?"

"Yes, yes!" Dog woofed. "A BIG boat!"

Fox smiled a bemused smile. "I have to confess that I have always wanted to ride on a boat. A salty breeze blowing through my fur. A jaunty sailor's cap on my head. Yes, it sounds like heaven." And then he raised his eyebrows and lowered his voice. "The only problem is that we are miles and miles away from the sea. Has your master thought of that?"

"Yes, yes!" Dog woofed. "He has thought of that. You see, we won't be going to the sea. The sea will be coming to us. Sort of. See?"

Fox sighed. "No, I don't see. And I especially don't see how the sea will be coming to us."

"Sort of," Dog woofed. "I said, 'Sort of.'"

"And how exactly will that happen, then? 'Sort of'?" Fox replied.

"It's going to rain!" Dog woofed. "Rain and

rain and rain! And rain."

Fox shifted his other paw to his other cheek. "Rain?" he repeated, incredulously. "Rain here? In what most people would call a desert?"

"That's right, that's right!" Dog woofed. "Rain hard enough to float a boat?"

"A big boat!" Dog woofed. "Very big! Big enough to carry two of every animal in the world!"

Fox tried not to laugh. "I'm working very hard to be polite," he sniggered. "But your master's idea is sounding more and more absurd. A boat big enough to carry two of every animal in the world would have to be enormous, for a start – assuming that you could collect two of every animal in the world. And to float that boat, you would need so much rain that everything we see around us would have to disappear beneath the water."

"I know, I know!" Dog woofed.

"I'm pleased to hear it," Fox replied. "Your loyalty has not blinded you to reason and common sense."

"No, no!" Dog woofed. "I know that it would take an enormous boat. And I know that it would take an even enormous-er flood. But that's what's going to happen. And that's why I'm here. So you can get on the boat and be safe!"

"I'm touched," said Fox. "I truly am. We have had our differences over the years – mostly to do with those chickens – so your concern for my well-being is particularly moving. But I won't be moving, from this spot *or* onto this enormous boat of yours, because your master's idea is, quite frankly, crackers."

"Oh, it wasn't his idea," Dog woofed. "Not his idea at all!"

"That is a relief," Fox sighed. "I was worried, for a moment there, that his insanity might affect you personally. That he would insist on calling you 'Plumcake' or dress you up in children's clothing. So whose idea was it, then?"

"God's!" Dog woofed. "It was God's idea."

Fox rolled his eyes. "Hmm. Well. Yes. I should have guessed."

"So you talk to God, too?" Dog woofed.

9

"No," Fox sighed. "I do not talk to God, my friend. Because there is no such person."

Dog stopped bouncing up and down. "No such person?" he woofed. "No such person? But my master talks to him all the time."

"Perhaps he does," Fox nodded. "Just as I talked to my imaginary friend, Basil, when I was a cub. But even then I knew that Basil was not real."

"How?" Dog woofed. "How?"

"Well, for a start," Fox replied, "he never talked back."

"Then that's the difference," Dog woofed. "That's the difference! God talks back to my master."

Fox sighed even more deeply. "Your master may think God talks back… Plumcake. But it's all in his imagination. Trust me."

"But God told him how to make the boat," Dog woofed. "How long and how high and how wide. And even what kind of wood to use. He was very specific!"

Fox shifted paws again. "And you don't think he just made it up, on his own?"

"He's never built a boat in his life!" Dog woofed. "But God… God made the whole world and everything in it. So surely he would know how to build a boat!"

"Made the world?" Fox mused. "That would be one explanation I suppose… if there were a God."

"So how do you think we got here?" asked Dog.

Fox shook his head. "Don't know. Not really bothered, actually. Maybe it all happened by chance. But I don't think it was because some Big Person in the Sky just magicked us here."

"Why not?" Dog woofed. "Why not?"

"Because a Big Person in the Sky would probably have done a better job of things," Fox replied. "He would have made chickens without feathers, for a start. That would have saved a lot of gagging."

"You're just being silly," Dog woofed. "Just silly."

"I'm not," said Fox. And he looked very serious. "Apart from your mildly bonkers master – who, I must admit, strikes me as a decent sort of fellow – have you spent much time with any humans lately?"

"Well, I spend time with my master's wife and their three sons and their wives," Dog woofed. "And they are all very nice to me."

"Yes, yes," Fox sighed. "Apart from your wannabe-sailor master and his extended wannabe-sailors family, do you have any other contact with humans?"

"Not so much," Dog woofed. "Not so much."

"Well, I do," Fox explained. "And even in my relatively short lifespan, I have seen them do the most violent and wicked things to each other. Unspeakably horrible things. Not to mention what they do to animals. And the longer I live, the worse it seems to get. Now what kind of God would make creatures who do things like that?"

Dog scratched his head. And his tail. "Dunno. But that's why he's sending the flood."

Fox crawled up out of his hole and looked Dog right in his dog face.

"GOD is sending the flood? Is that what you're telling me? Or, rather, is that what your master believes?"

"That's what God TOLD him," Dog woofed. "God said

that people had got so violent and were doing such awful things to each other that he was sorry he had made them. And that he wanted to start over again."

"By drowning everybody?" Fox's eyebrows were raised again.

"Well, not everybody," Dog woofed. "Not my master, Noah. And not his family either. And not the animals who are on the boat. Like me. And you." And then he whispered, "If you come."

"But why Noah?" Fox asked. "Why does he get special treatment?"

"You said it yourself," Dog woofed, "just a minute ago. He's not like the other humans you know. And I guess God knows that, too."

Fox sat back on his haunches and stared at the ground.

"So what you're saying is that God – assuming there is a God – is going to save the world by destroying it?"

Dog looked at the ground too. "Or maybe he's going to save the world from destroying itself by saving a little piece of it. Just enough to start again with." Then he lifted up his head and looked at Fox. "I was just sort of hoping that you'd be a piece of that little piece."

Fox smiled. "I'm flattered. I really am. But I'm also a fox. And I don't have to tell you what that means. I trust my brain. I survive on my cleverness. It's reason that counts in my world. And my brain tells me that, nice as you are, you and your master are on a fool's errand. I don't see any harm coming from it – apart from you frightening those who believe in your message. And the possibility, of course, that one of the larger animals you have invited onto your boat might decide that it's a Dinner Cruise and choose you as the main course. No, I think I'll decline your invitation. But do have a wonderful time on your pretend trip, in the pretend rain, sent by your pretend god."

Dog looked sad. Very sad.

"So you're saying no just because you think you're smarter than me?"

Fox cleared his throat. "I'm very sorry, my friend, but yes, I am smarter than you. As are dolphins. And pigs. And several other species. Cats, surely.

"I have outwitted you more times than I can count. We're back to chickens again. So why not trust my judgment in this matter, too?"

"Because I'm not stupid," Dog woofed. "I may not be as clever as you, but I'm using my brain, too. I trust my master. He has never let me down. I know that. And I know that people are getting worse and worse – you said it yourself. That's evidence that there is truth to my master's story. And even though I can't prove there is a God or that he talked to my master, my master has never done anything crazy before and has never lied to me. So I'm using my brain. And I'm using something else. I'm using what a dog is good at. I'm using my loyalty – my trust in the people who love me. And if they're getting on the boat, then I'm getting on with them."

"Fair enough," said Fox, turning around. "I'll come knock on the door in a few days, shall I? You'll have chickens on board, surely?"

"I don't feel like joking anymore," woofed Dog sadly. "Goodbye, my friend."

Then Fox crawled back into his hole.

And Dog climbed onto the boat.

The Counsellor's Version

The Tower of Babel

The woman and her son walked tentatively into the tent. They looked around, nervously, and finally sat themselves down.

Music was playing softly in the background. Some kind of whistle or pipe, the woman thought.

And then, after a few moments, the counsellor pulled back the tent flap and joined them.

"What seems to be the problem, Mrs... Arphaxad?" he asked, glancing at his clay appointment tablet.

Mrs Arphaxad sighed. "It's Obal, my son, here. We don't seem to be able to communicate anymore."

The counsellor looked at the boy, and Obal just grunted, lowered his shaggy head, and rested his chin on his chest.

"And for how long has this been going on?" asked the counsellor.

"Oh, not long at all," said Mrs Arphaxad. "Since just yesterday, in fact – when he turned thirteen."

"I see." The counsellor smiled, leaning back and making a little tent shape with his fingers. "Since he became a teenager, in other words. Well, it's not uncommon, Mrs Arphaxad. I see this a lot. One day – a bright and happy boy. And the next day – well, we can see for ourselves."

Obal grunted and his mum shook her head.

"I don't think it's as simple as that," she replied. "I think there's more to it. I really do!"

"Raging hormones.

Teenage angst. The sudden eruption of spots. I should think that's reason enough, Mrs Arphaxad." And he peeped at his hourglass. "But we do have quite a bit of sand left, if you want to tell me what you think the reason is."

"I think it has to do with something that happened at work," she replied.

"Hmm," nodded the counsellor. "What do you think, Obal?"

And Obal just grunted and shrugged.

"I'm not sure if that's a 'yes' or a 'no'," said the counsellor.

"My problem exactly," Mrs Arphaxad replied. "And it's even worse when he speaks. I can't understand a thing he says!"

The counsellor smiled once more. "Again, not an unusual problem, Mrs Arphaxad. Teenagers have always had their own special phrases. 'Groovy.' 'Slip me some skin.'"

"Yes, well, I think it's more than the odd word," the woman insisted. "As I said, it all seems to have started…"

"At work, yes," the counsellor interrupted. "So you said. So why don't you tell me exactly what happened?" And then he paused, irritated.

"Do you think that music's a little loud?" he asked.

"Now that you mention it, yes." Mrs Arphaxad replied.

So the counsellor reached back and pulled a flap aside.

"A tad quieter, Peleg," he ordered the musician sitting there.

And then he turned his attention back to his clients.

"You were saying…" he continued.

Mrs Arphaxad shifted in her seat, collected herself, and began:

"I run a little mobile snack bar at the big building site on the edge of the city."

"Where they're putting up that new tower?" asked the counsellor.

"That's right," nodded Mrs Arphaxad. "And Obal here comes in and gives me a hand after school. He makes the drinks and does the washing up, and it provides him with a bit of pocket money.

"Well, if I do say so myself, we have built up a bit of a reputation. Bacon rolls in the morning. Freshly prepared sandwiches at lunch. And all our cakes are homemade."

"Sounds very nice," the counsellor noted.

"It is!" smiled Mrs Arphaxad. "So much so, that we had a visit from Mr Shinar himself – the man in charge of building the tower!"

"Very impressive," nodded the counsellor. And then he held up his hand and pulled back the tent flap again.

"Peleg!" he shouted. "I told you to keep it down!" The counsellor turned back around but the musician just shrugged and kept on playing.

"Musicians," he sighed. "Temperamental. You were saying?"

Mrs Arphaxad leaned forward, grinning. "I was saying that Mr Shinar himself came to visit our little snack bar. Obal made him a lovely cup of tea, and he had one of my cheese scones. Then, when he took the time to compliment me on my cookery skills, I summoned up all my courage and asked him how he thought the tower was going.

"Well, it was like a proper conversation – like he had known me for ages.

" 'Ahh, Mrs Arphaxad,' he said – knew me by name, he did! 'Ahh, Mrs Arphaxad, the tower project is going well beyond all expectations. We intend to make a reputation for ourselves, we do. We're using bricks instead of

stone. We're using tar for mortar. Everyone's on the same page. Everyone's speaking the same language. And, as a result, we believe that this tower will reach right to heaven and give God himself a bit of competition!' "

Mrs Arphaxad leaned forward even further. "To be honest," she whispered, "that last bit did make me a tad nervous. Right up to heaven. Makes you wonder what God would think."

"Well, you'll have to ask a priest about that," the counsellor grinned. "Not really my area, if you know what I mean. But what does any of this have to do with your son's lack of communication?"

"I'm not exactly sure," said Mrs Arphaxad. "It's just that the moment Mr Shinar left, it happened. I turned to Obal and asked him to pass me a butter knife. And he just looked at me, like he hadn't a clue in the world what I was on about. I asked him again – and that's when all the grunting and shrugging started."

"So it happened immediately?" asked the counsellor.

"Just like that," Mrs Arphaxad replied. "It was very strange."

So the counsellor turned again to the boy.

"You need to help us, here, Obal. You really do. I understand how difficult it can be to make

that transition from boy to young man. Why, I've been there myself. But you can see how distraught your mother is. Can you give us some tiny clue as to what's going on inside of you, or how we might help?"

And that's when the boy raised his shaggy head. He looked at the counsellor. He looked at his mum. And then, very deliberately, he spoke.

"Iway an'tcay understandway away ingthay ou'reyay ayingsay."

The counsellor looked worried.

"Hmm. Can't make head nor tail of that. I see exactly what you mean." And then he paused. "Mind you, it would help if the music weren't playing and I could hear what was going on!" And he opened the tent flap again.

"For the last time, Peleg!" he shouted. "Could you keep the music down!"

Once again the musician shrugged. But this time, he put down his flute and he spoke.

"Iway an'tcay understandway away

ingthay ou'reyay ayingsay."

The counsellor turned white as a sheet.

"Did you hear that?" he cried. "Whatever is going on with your son seems to have affected Peleg as well!"

Mrs Arphaxad put her hands to her face in horror. "You don't suppose it's catching?" she asked.

But Obal was jumping up and down, delighted, and pointing at the musician.

The counsellor pointed as well, first to Peleg and then to his mouth. And then, speaking as loudly as he could, he asked the boy, "DO YOU UNDERSTAND HIM?"

"He's not deaf!" complained Mrs Arphaxad, as the boy kept hopping and nodding and pointing.

"Well, I'm taking it as a 'yes'," replied the counsellor. "And that means we've got some kind of strange language affliction thing going on here. Something well beyond my expertise. I think we need a specialist."

And he opened a different flap and called for his receptionist.

"Miss Joktan, I need you to get in touch with Dr Hadoram. Immediately."

But the receptionist just stuck her head through the flap, a confused look on her face.

"Que?" she answered. "No comprendo."

"Right then," said the counsellor, leaping from his seat and collecting his things. "Time for me to go now, Mrs Arphaxad. Pleased to have met you. Sorry I couldn't have been more help. All the best to you and your son. Arrivederci!"

And, shocked, he put his hand over his mouth and raced out of the tent and down the street.

Mrs Arphaxad followed, with Obal and Peleg in tow, chatting away to each other.

There was chaos, everywhere. Everyone jibber-jabbering to each other with words they could not understand.

And rising high into the sky, in the middle of it all, stood the tower, half-finished.

Mrs Arphaxad looked up at the tower – and beyond it, to the clouds.

"Competing with God himself?" she wondered. "Hmm..."

Then she turned to her son and gestured,

"Let's go." And she waved for him to bring Peleg along as well.

"Might as well get some food into you," she said, pretending to shove something into her mouth.

Obal looked at Peleg. "Eeseychay onesscay," he grinned.

"Umyay!" Peleg replied.

And they headed for their snack bar, in the shadow of the tower, as everyone babbled around them.

Grandad's Version

Elijah and the Prophets of Baal

My grandad leaned back against the wall and looked at the ceiling.

"I suppose I've always been a fan of the underdog," he mused.

I could feel a story coming. I searched in vain for a way out. But Mum was making dinner and I had a pile of vegetables to chop. So I was stuck.

"When I was your age, young Malachi, I was sport mad. But it was always the underdog I supported. And I have no regrets."

"So what football team was it, then?" I asked. It seemed the polite thing to do. And the pile of veggies was huge.

"Football?" he snorted. "Football! Why, we didn't have those fancy shmancy footballs in my day, boy. Balls made of skin – stuffed and sewn together? You don't know how lucky you are."

"So what did you kick?" I asked.

"Coneys, boy! Rock badgers! We'd catch one of those critters, set him in the middle of the pitch, and see who could kick him to the other side."

"Sounds cruel to me," said my mum.

"And so it was!" replied Grandad. "Those little beasties could bite! You'd put your boot in – but of course we didn't have boots in those days, just our bare feet – and the coney would clamp his teeth around your big toe. I can't begin to describe the pain."

"Well, maybe if you hadn't been trying to kick them…" I suggested.

"My point exactly, boy. The underdog! Or rather the under-coney. That's whose side I was on. So one day, when my mates were chasing one of the little critters, I swooped in, scooped him up off the ground, and just started running with him. And when I stumbled into the goal, everyone cheered and picked me up and hoisted me onto their shoulders."

"Because you saved the coney?" asked my mum.

"No! Because I'd inadvertently invented a new way of playing the game. My mates were fed up with having their toes gnawed, so they changed the rules. And from that point on, you could either Kick the Coney or Carry the Coney."

"But didn't the coneys just bite your thumbs instead of your toes?" I asked.

"You're getting ahead of me, boy," he scowled. "Never get ahead of an old man and his story."

"Sorry," I muttered.

"And yes," he continued. "They did bite our thumbs – and that resulted in my final innovation, Tossing the Coney. It was a natural reaction at first. They'd chomp on your thumb – you'd chuck them in the air. But before long, coneys were flying all over the field – as a proper part of the game."

"And they liked that better than being kicked or carried?" asked my mum.

"The flying, yes," Grandad smiled. "You could see the expressions of delight and joy on their little coney faces."

Then he shook his head. "But the landing, not so much."

"Well, I'm glad we just kick balls today,"
I said.

"And that we have water," added Grandad.

"Water?" said my mum.

"That's right. In my day there was a drought so bad that it didn't rain for three whole years. Dirt. That's all we had. Dirt plates and dirt spoons and dirt houses and dirt sandwiches – or maybe they were made of sand, I forget. It was something we scraped off the ground."

"When was that, Grandad?"

"The Days of Elijah,"
he nodded. "Those were
the days. Of Elijah."

31

"He was a prophet, wasn't he?" said my mum.

"One of the best prophets Israel ever had," Grandad replied. "In fact, they say that he was the one who stopped the rain. Well, God did it, I suppose – but it was Elijah that told evil King Ahab and even evil-er Queen Jezebel that it was going to happen."

"Why were they evil?" I asked.

"Because they got our people to stop worshipping the true God and to worship Baal instead."

"Baal?" I said.

"That's right, Baal," Grandad nodded. "It rhymes with 'pail'. Although some folks insist that it's actually Baal, which rhymes with… well… 'ball'. It's confusing really – but all you need to know is that he was some foreign fertility god."

"Fertility?" I asked. And Grandad blushed.

"Erm… you'll have to ask your mum about that," he muttered.

Mum looked at Grandad and shook

her head. Then said, matter-of-factly, "They believed he made the crops grow."

I scratched my head. "But I thought the true God of Israel did that."

"And so he does, boy," Grandad grinned. "But in those days – the Days of Elijah – there weren't many of us who believed that. So Elijah arranged a little competition, between himself and the prophets of Baal, to prove whose god was more powerful. And I'm sure you can guess whose side I was rooting for."

"The coneys'?" I answered.

"No! The underdog's! Elijah – that's who I supported. Don't know where this fixation with coneys came from."

"But you…"

"Don't interrupt an old man in the middle of his story, boy. Now where was I? Oh, yeah – four hundred and fifty. That's how many prophets of Baal there were. And only one Elijah.

"The competition was held at the top of Mount Carmel. Each side had a bull and a pile of wood. The bulls were killed and chopped up into pieces and placed on the wood…"

"More animal cruelty," sighed my mum.

"And then each side was given the chance to call on their god to send fire down from heaven and burn up the bulls!"

"That sounds amazing!" I gasped. "Were you there?"

"Everybody was there!" Grandad beamed. "But most of the people, my mates included, were supporting the Baals.

"They had big Bs painted on their chests and waved bright Baal banners and even chanted their noisy Baal songs.

"I can remember it like it was yesterday. 'Baal, Baal, he can't fail!'

"Or in the case of those who preferred the alternative pronunciation, 'Baal, Baal, he can't fall!'

"Honestly, if you're going to worship a deity, you ought to be able to agree on how to say his name."

"But what did your mates do when they found out that you supported the God of Israel?" I asked.

"What do you think?" he sighed. "They called me names. They laughed at me. They threw things at me. Things made of dirt, mostly."

"And coneys?" I suggested.

Grandad scowled. "You're making me sorry I brought that up, boy. But, yes, there was the odd airborne coney. So I just stood off by myself, waving my little 'Go Jehovah!' flag. And then I caught Elijah's eye."

"Did he wave to you or anything?" I asked.

"More than that," Grandad grinned. "He came over to me. He thanked me for my support. He told me that there were hundreds just like me who supported him too. And that if we walked through the storm, and kept our chins up high, and weren't afraid of the dark, and held hope in our hearts, that we would never walk alone."

"You'll never walk alone." said my mum, brushing a tear from her eye. "That's very moving."

"So what happened?" I said. "Who won?"

"You're getting ahead of me again, boy," Grandad muttered. "This is a story worth telling one step at a time.

"The prophets of Baal went first…"

"They must have won the coney toss," I chuckled.

"The prophets of Baal went first," he repeated, ignoring my remark. "And they prayed to their god all morning, dancing around the bull. But nothing happened. Not a thing. So Elijah started to taunt them. You know, make fun of them.

" 'Maybe you need to shout louder,' he suggested. 'Maybe Baal's deep in thought. Maybe he's busy. Maybe he's on holiday. Maybe

he's gone for a wee.'"

"I bet that made your mates angry," I said.

"My mates? Yeah, they were angry all right. But that was nothing compared to the prophets of Baal. They grabbed their swords and spears and started cutting themselves. They shouted louder and louder. There was noise and there was blood and…"

"I think that's enough, Dad," suggested my mum. "We get the idea."

"All right then," he sighed. "I was just painting a picture for the boy. It's not like we saw intestines or anything…"

"Dad!"

"Or spleens," he muttered. "All right, it was messy. We'll leave it at that. The point is that nothing happened. Baal didn't answer. So Elijah told everyone to come to him. He took twelve stones, one for each of the tribes of Israel, and repaired an old altar to God that had been broken down. He put the wood and the bull pieces on the altar. And then he dug a trench around the altar."

"A trench?" I said. "What for?"

Grandad chuckled. "You won't believe it. My mates didn't, that's for sure. He told someone to fill four big jars with water and dump them on the bull and on the wood."

"The wood that was supposed to catch fire?" I asked.

"That's right," Grandad nodded.

"And all that water – in a drought?" added my mum. "What a waste."

Grandad nodded again. "And what a risk. You could hear the people moaning."

"So what did Elijah do?" I asked.

"The same thing again," Grandad answered. "More jugs. More water. And then he did it a

THIRD time! And there was so much water on the altar that it ran down and filled up the trench.

"Now it was my mates who were laughing. There was no way that mess was going to catch fire. And they knew it.

"But Elijah didn't seem bothered at all. He stepped forward, he looked to heaven, and he prayed:

" 'Lord of Abraham, Isaac, and Jacob, show these people that you are the true God. Answer my prayer so that they will turn back to you.' "

"And then?" I said. "Then what happened?"

"Then he winked at me, boy. Me and my little 'Go Jehovah!' flag. And before I could wave back or anything, fire fell from heaven. Fire so hot and so fierce that it burned up the bull and the wood and the stones and the soil and every bit of water in that trench!"

"Wow! And what did your friends do?"

"They fell on their faces, with everybody else on that mountain, and cried, 'The Lord – he is God! The Lord – he is God!' Well, everybody but the four hundred and fifty prophets of Baal. They thought it might be a good time to exit the pitch."

"So they got away?"

"Nah. The people hunted them down and

killed them all."

"A bit extreme," noted my mum.

"It was a different era," Grandad shrugged. "Relegation hadn't been invented yet."

"Well, thanks for the story," said my mum. "And you can stay for dinner, if you like."

"Much appreciated," Grandad replied, "but I need to stretch my legs." Then he turned to me. "I wouldn't mind a bit of that turnip you've been chopping up, though."

"Sure," I said. And I tossed him a piece. "But it's not cooked."

"Oh, it's not for me," he chuckled. And he reached into his pocket and pulled out… a coney!

"Who's been a good boy, then?" he coo-ed, stroking the coney under its chin. "And here's a little treat for you."

Then Grandad stood up, the coney nibbled on the turnip, and they walked out of the house.

And the last thing I heard was, "Owww! That's not a turnip, that's my thumb! I think somebody needs to do a little flying. Wheeeeee…!"

The Swineherd's Version

Jesus Heals a Man with Demons

My dad and I walked into the room and sat down. The man on the other side of the table looked very serious.

He didn't speak to us at first. I looked at my dad. My dad looked at me. I shuffled my feet. He folded and unfolded his hands. Neither of us knew what to expect.

Finally, the man smiled. But I wouldn't say that it was a friendly smile, exactly. More like something he was supposed to do.

"Now, then," he said. "My name is Mr Balak.

And I work for the Ten Towns Mutual Assurance Company. And you are… Farmer Swine?"

"That's right," my dad nodded.

"And this is…?" he asked, looking at me.

"My son. Swine Junior. He was there, on the day. The day of the attack."

"Yes. Well," said Mr Balak, "that is why we are here, isn't it? Because of what you call the 'attack'."

"I've already told the other man everything that happened," said my dad, defensively. "It was an attack. My pigs were killed. I don't know what else there is to say."

"Let's go over the details of the case," said Mr Balak. "And then, perhaps, you will understand why I have called this meeting."

Dad was sweating. He always sweated when he was nervous. "Sweated like a pig." That's what he'd always say. And given his job and our name, that was funny. But it wasn't funny now.

Mr Balak cleared his throat and began:

"As I understand it, you say that your entire herd of pigs plunged off a hill, at the edge of your property, into the sea, where they drowned. Furthermore, you say that this was the fault of a Jewish rabbi called Jesus, who was standing in a cemetery at the seaside below."

"That's right," my dad nodded. "That's exactly what happened."

"Hmm," muttered Mr Balak. "We shall see. Now then, your insurance policy does, indeed, cover acts of violence toward your herd. However, we have been unable to uncover any evidence that proves your claim to be true.

"Granted, some of your neighbours saw a

43

rabbi and his followers at the seaside that day, but no one saw him approach your herd or attempt to disturb it in any way. He did not have a stick. There were no dogs present. Nothing, in fact, that could be used to chase even one pig off a cliff, much less an entire herd."

"I never said the man used a stick!" my dad replied. "It was unusual, what Jesus did, yes – but it was his fault. You talked to my witness, didn't you?"

Mr Balak nodded. And harrumphed. "Your witness? Yes, we did interview the witness that you suggested to us. And he did tell us a story similar to the one we heard from you.

"He explained that he was wandering among the tombs when Jesus and his disciples suddenly appeared on the shore. He described how he approached Jesus and how Jesus then cast a collection ('legion' is the word he used) of demons out of him and into your herd of pigs. And, according to him, that is why they then leaped to their watery doom."

"There you go," grinned my dad, slamming his hand on the table. "It was Jesus' fault! My witness saw him do it. Now all you need to do is pay me what my herd was worth, and my son and I will be on our way."

"Sadly, it is not as simple as that," replied Mr Balak. And now there was nothing even approaching a smile on his face.

"I know you believe that this should have convinced us of the truth of your case. The only problem, Farmer Swine, is that you failed to tell us that your witness was a madman!

"Nutcase. Lunatic. Bonkers. That is how your neighbours describe this witness, Farmer Swine. According to our sources, he has spent much of the last few years of his life among the tombs. Naked – because of his illness. And chained – we can only guess – so that his mad rages would not prove harmful to himself or to others.

"While it is true that he seemed perfectly 'normal' during our interview, our experts have told us that madmen are very good at pretending to be normal. So the story he told us

45

about Jesus and the demons could also have been a result of his madness. It certainly sounds 'mad' to me."

"But he's all right now," I blurted out. "Doesn't that count for something?"

They both turned and looked at me.

"Who is all right?" asked Mr Balak.

"The… the… madman," I answered. "He's not crazy any more. He doesn't have to be chained. He wears clothes. Doesn't that mean you should trust what he says?"

"Young man," Mr Balak replied, looking down his nose at me. "Unless you are an expert in mental diseases as well as a swineherd, what you say is a matter of opinion, and opinion only. The man was not in his right mind when this so-called attack occurred. So how can his evidence be trusted? And speaking of 'mad'…"

And here he turned his withering gaze upon my dad.

"Let's talk about your own failure to provide fencing at the edge of the cliff. Demons or no demons, a good strong fence would have stopped your pigs from their deadly plunge – and they would be alive, rooting and snorting happily today."

Mr Balak folded his arms across his chest.

"No, Farmer Swine, in the absence of any

other witnesses, we are going to have to reject your claim. You are free, of course, to find this rabbi and sue him for damages in civil court. But we suspect that a judge would be as skeptical of your witness's account as we are.

"We are sorry for your loss. But you must understand that insurance fraud is common these days and costs everyone – company and customer alike. This is not to imply, in any way, that we suspect your motives. It is simply a sad fact that every claim must be dealt with thoroughly. And in your case, the facts do not add up. It is unfortunate that your pigs plunged from the cliff to their deaths. But we can see no connection between that event and any human action. In the end, we must chalk it up as an 'act of God' and leave it at that.

"If you have any further questions, do not hesitate to contact me at your convenience."

"So I don't get any money?" asked my dad.

"Not a fig, I'm afraid," replied Mr Balak. "As I think I have said clearly, your insurance policy covered an attack on your herd. And there simply was no attack."

"But… but… that was my whole living," my dad sighed. "What am I supposed to do now?"

"I'm afraid I have no answer for that," said Mr Balak, rising from the table. "But I do have another appointment. So if you will excuse me..." And he headed for the door.

I couldn't do it. I couldn't hold it in any longer.

"What if there were another witness?" I asked. "Someone who wasn't crazy?" And now I was sweating, too.

Mr Balak turned and looked at me.

"What other witness?" he asked.

"Me," I mumbled.

"You?" said my dad. "But you were up on the hill with the pigs! That's what you told me. You tried to stop them, but they ran right past you. That's what you said. Are you saying that you have been lying to me all this time?"

"Yes," I whispered.

"Sorry," I whispered, too. "I knew you'd be angry if you found out. I thought you'd blame me for the pigs. But I don't think I could have stopped them, anyway."

"That is not the point, young man," said Mr Balak, returning to his seat. "The point is: where were you?"

"Down in the cemetery," I confessed. "With... Colin... you know... the madman." I said. "Except he's not mad anymore, he really isn't!"

"But he was mad THEN!" said my dad.

"Yes, I suppose so," I shrugged. "But I knew

him, sort of. Well, as well as you can know any crazy naked chained-up person. I was on the hill every day, watching the pigs. And he was down there in the cemetery, doing his crazy naked thing. And at first I was just curious, so I went down there, and he sort of screamed at me for a bit. So I started leaving him bits of my lunch, which he liked. And then we got to saying 'Hi' and 'How are you doing?' and then 'Well, must be off, lots to do.'"

"Your mother will go spare when she finds out!" my dad shouted again.

"That's why I never said anything. I didn't want you to worry. He was chained up. I kept my distance. Like I said, I'm sorry."

Mr Balak cleared his throat. "Leaving your

family issues and returning to the point for a moment, what exactly did you see and hear, young man, when you were down in the cemetery?"

"Everything that Colin told you," I replied.

"All right, I was hiding behind a tomb, because I didn't know who the people in the boat were. But I peeped out from time to time, and I heard it all! Jesus told the demons that were in Colin to go into our herd of pigs."

"And you are certain that there were demons in Colin because..."

"Because they kept screaming, 'Jesus, Son of God, don't torture us! Jesus, don't send us into the abyss!' Like I said, I heard everything. And it was really scary!"

My dad looked at Mr Balak.

"So does this change anything?" he asked.

"There is a part of me," said Mr Balak, "that wants to be suspicious about this sudden turn of events. But there is another part of me that saw the look on your face when your son confessed that he was in the graveyard. A part that believes you were truly surprised. So I will give both you and he the benefit of the doubt. You will receive money to buy a replacement herd, Farmer Swine. But can I suggest that you use at least part of that fund to build yourself a sturdy fence?"

"And maybe hire myself a swineherd who doesn't have crazy friends," my dad added, looking at me.

"No worries, Dad," I said. "I'll never leave the herd again. Promise."

"I'd take his word for that," said Mr Balak. "After all, in the end, he did save your bacon." And he shook my hand and my dad's hand and smiled. A real smile this time.

My dad smiled, too. And why shouldn't he? The Swines had pigs again!

The Professional Mourner's Version

Jesus Raises the Dead

I'd never heard such wailing in my life. Which is saying something, really, seeing as wailing was my job. Or would have been, one day. I was an apprentice, you see, at Lamentations Limited, the nation's most famous firm of professional mourners.

"You die. We cry." That was our motto. So whenever anyone passed away, we got the call to join the family and weep along with them. There was usually a bit of breast-beating and garment-tearing as well – anything to show how upset you were at the loss of your loved one. The rule was: the more upset you were, the more noise you made – and the more noise you made, the more you loved the one who died. So we got paid to make everything as noisy as possible.

Which is why I was surprised at the volume of the wailing that greeted me when I walked up to the office. Practices were never at full volume, so either one of our own had died or we were all getting the sack.

The minute I walked in, though, it all stopped. And six pairs of eyes looked at me.

"So where have you been?" moaned Martha, who actually was a "moaner". It's an important speciality – that sort of continuous, low-end thrum at the bottom of the grieving package.

"I was out of town. At my aunt's," I shrugged. "I just got back. Did I miss something?"

"MISS SOMETHING!" shrieked Shirley, who, true to her job description, forced me to put my fingers in my ears. "ONLY THE WORST THING THAT'S HAPPENED TO US IN YEARS!"

"It's that Jesus again," sighed Sarah, like the world was about to end.

"You mean the rabbi?" I asked.

"OF COURSE WE MEAN THE RABBI!" shrieked Shirley. And a ceramic pot shattered somewhere on the far side of the room.

"It's all right, dear," whispered Sylvia, sympathetically, as she took my hand. "You're new. We understand." And there were tears in her eyes. But then, there were always tears in her eyes. That was her job. To be compassionate, understanding, and... well... sympathetic.

"She's only an apprentice," moaned Martha. "Nothing more than a sniffler. How could she possibly understand?"

Martha was right, of course. I was just a sniffler. But sniffling was where everyone started. And basic as it may be, it brought a

depth to the occasion. The watery eyes, the handkerchief, the runny nose, the little strand of snot. People appreciated it, I think. And I took pride in the contribution I made.

"So what's the matter with Jesus?" I sniffled, rubbing my nose with the back of my hand for effect. "As far as I've heard, he does good things. Making blind people see. Making lame people walk…"

"And making dead people alive again," sighed Sarah, as if that were the worst thing that could possibly happen.

"It started nearly three years ago!" wept Wilma, who seemed genuinely weepy. "Up in G..G..G…" She was struggling to control herself.

"Galilee," said Sylvia, finishing the sentence and taking hold of Wilma's hand as a gesture of support.

"There was a widow whose boy died," moaned Martha, as if she was the widow herself. "And Jesus showed up during the funeral procession."

"He t..t..t..t..touched the casket," wept Wilma.

"And brought the boy back to life again," Sarah sighed.

"That sounds like a good thing," I suggested.

"THE WIDOW WANTED HER MONEY BACK!" shrieked Shirley. "OUR PEOPLE WERE THERE. THEY WEPT. THEY WAILED. THEY MOURNED. THEY SHOWED THE UTMOST PROFESSIONALISM. BUT BECAUSE THE BOY WAS ALIVE AGAIN, HIS MOTHER WANTED HER MONEY BACK!!"

"I see," I sniffled. And I really did. Shirley could be truly frightening. "So it's sort of about profit?"

A low growl emanated from the far

56

corner of the room. Anna had been quiet to this point. I'd forgotten she was there. But anger, they say, is one of the necessary stages of grief. And Anna could do "anger" like nobody else I knew.

"It's not about profit," she growled. And I have no idea how she managed to do that voice. It hardly sounded human. "It's about pride in one's work. It's about honouring one's position. It's about respect!"

"And if Jesus had just kept his nose out of it," moaned Martha, "then everything would have been all right."

I scratched my head, confused. "But the boy would have still been dead," I said.

Sylvia took hold of my hand, a single tear trickling down her cheek. "I can see how you might look at it that way, dear. But you have to consider the other outcomes. The widow was, indeed, given a refund, and as a result, our employer had to let a few of us go. We lost two eye-daubers and one of our best breast-beaters."

"A tragedy," sighed Sarah. "Truly a tragedy."

Wilma started weeping again. "And then… and then… and then… there was that business up in C..C..C..Capernaum." She blew her nose and, then, something ripped.

Personally, I've never understood garment-rending. Seems a waste of a perfectly decent dress. But I guess the point is that if you're upset enough to tear up something you paid good money for, then you're pretty upset. It's hard going, though, ripping up all that cloth, so Gomer, our chief garment-render, conserved as much energy as possible. Well, that's the official explanation. I just think she liked to nap. But she wasn't napping anymore.

"The dead girl was the daughter of Jairus." Riiiiiip!

"An official in the synagogue. Our people were there, just doing their job. When this Jesus shows up. And says she's only sleeping. I know a dead person when I see one. And so does everyone else who works for this firm. And so someone laughed at his suggestion." Riiiiiiip!

"NOOOOOOOOOOOO!" shrieked Shirley. "NOOOOOOOOOOOOOOOOOOOOOOOOO!"

Everyone covered their ears and hit the floor. Pottery exploded across the room. And the dog clawed its way out the front door.

Shirley finally stopped. And passed out. Sylvia took my hand again (it was starting to creep me out). And now there were tears running down both cheeks. And a little blood trickling out of one ear. She might actually have been in pain.

"You understand the problem, dear? Do you?"

I nodded. "It's the prime directive, isn't it? The thing that must never, ever happen. A professional mourner. Laughing."

"That's right, dear," Sylvia replied, her grip a vice on my hand. "Sometimes family members will laugh. It's down to nervousness, mostly. But we must always, in every circumstance, maintain a sorrowful disposition. It's just good form. And I am afraid, on that occasion, that all semblance of proper decorum was lost."

"I blame the rabbi," Anna growled. And there was a great deal of nodding and moaning and sighing and ripping, etcetera, in reply.

"If he hadn't made such a ridiculous suggestion," she continued, "it would never

have happened. And more good workers would not have been lost."

"They couldn't be trusted after that," moaned Martha.

"And the daughter?" I dared to ask.

"She lived," Sarah sighed. "So maybe she WAS just sleeping."

"Or maybe he brought her back from the dead," I suggested. "Like he did with the widow's son."

Wilma started weeping again. "The p..p..p.. point is that he's not up in Galilee any longer. He's here, in B..B..B.. Bethany. Just up the road!"

"And he's up to his old tricks," growled Anna.

"What? Raising people from the dead?" I asked.

"I'm afraid so," whispered Sylvia, wrapping her arm around my shoulder. "It's bad news, I know. But it has to be faced."

"But it's not…," I started to say.

"Not the end of the world, dear," said Sylvia, patting me on the head. "Yes, I'm certain of that. We all are. But we must be vigilant."

"The dead man's name was Lazarus," said Gomer with a riiiiiip!

"He was one of Jesus' friends," sighed Sarah. "And he was very ill."

"The man's sisters begged for Jesus to come," moaned Martha.

"But he stayed away and let his friend die," Anna growled.

"To be fair," added Sylvia, "they do say he stayed away so that he could demonstrate the power of God."

"In any case," said Gomer. Riiiiiip! "Lazarus was buried."

"They used another firm of mourners," Sarah sighed.

"The Dead Body Shop," moaned Martha.

"Amateurs," Anna growled.

And now Wilma was weeping again. "J..J.. Jesus asked one of the sisters if she believed that she would see her brother again. The woman said, 'Yes, on the last day, when the dead are raised.' And then Jesus said the most t..t.. terrifying thing."

" 'I AM THE RESURRECTION AND THE

LIFE!' " shrieked Shirley, popping up from the floor like she had popped up out of the grave. " 'WHOEVER BELIEVES IN ME WILL LIVE, EVEN IF HE DIES. AND WHOEVER LIVES BY BELIEVING IN ME WILL NEVER DIE!' "

"Never die?" moaned Martha. "Don't you see? If no one ever dies, we're ruined!"

"And if people know their loved ones will live again," sighed Sarah, "and they'll see them, what's the point of grieving?"

" 'Cause they'll miss them in the meantime, surely," I argued.

"There wasn't much 'meantime' for Lazarus and his sisters," growled Anna. "Jesus saw to that!"

Gomer tore her dress with one long dramatic riiiiiiip!

"He told them to roll the stone away from the front of Lazarus' tomb."

"They say the smell was overwhelming," moaned Martha.

"And then Jesus said the words," sighed Sarah.

"What words?" I asked.

Sylvia whispered it in my ear. " 'Lazarus, come out.' "

"AND HE DID!" shrieked Shirley. "HE WALKED OUT OF THE TOMB, ALIVE, ALL

COVERED IN GRAVECLOTHES. HE DID! HE WAS ALIVE!"

And that's when it happened. That's when I violated the prime directive. That's when I started to laugh.

"I'm sorry," I apologized. "I really am. I know you all find this news upsetting, but this is just about the best thing I have ever heard! An end to death? A future that lasts forever? Resurrection and life? I think I want some of that."

"Then you had better turn in your hankie," said Sylvia coldly, removing her arm from my shoulder and her hand from mine.

So I did. And as the room filled again with weeping and shrieking and ripping and sighing and moaning and growling, I walked out of the office and headed for home.

And I wondered. With this thing that Jesus was doing – resurrection and life – might there possibly be an opening for a Professional Laugher?

The Nephew's Version

Judas Agrees to Betray Jesus

I turned the corner, and there he was, in the alley. My Uncle J!

"Uncle J!" I called. "Uncle J!"

He didn't turn around at first, so I kept calling. And finally, he whipped round with his finger to his mouth.

"Quiet, Simon!"

He used to be a revolutionary, my Uncle J. Part of this underground movement that wanted to overthrow the Romans and kick them out of our country. He had a really cool

65

knife and everything, which he kept hidden under his robes. He'd sneak up behind a soldier or a Roman official maybe. He'd pull out that knife and *snick*, game over for the Roman! I wished he'd never left. I mean I couldn't tell my friends or anything, but to have an uncle who was sort of like a spy. Amazing!

"So are you murdering Romans again?" I whispered.

He shook his head. "No. There are just some people I need to… avoid." Then he pushed me away. "You should go home."

I was disappointed. "Is it because you're all religious now? Working for that Jesus?"

Uncle J sighed. "I don't work for him. I'm one of his disciples. It's like a training programme for rabbis…"

I just stared at him, blank-faced. Killing Roman soldiers was cool. Training to be a rabbi – not so much.

"Look, just go home!" he repeated.

And that's when the two men walked up behind him. I saw them first and thought they might be some of his old friends. They definitely looked like killers. They had big chests and big arms and big scars.

One of them grabbed Uncle J, slammed him against a wall, and put a knife to his throat. The

other one put his hand around my neck. Really!
One hand! Right around my neck!

Not exactly friends, then.

"Listen up, Iscariot," the one with the knife
growled. "We want the money. Now!"

"I haven't got it," said Uncle J. "I told your
boss. He said he'd give me more time."

"He thought you were broke, Iscariot," the
other one growled. "But we've been following
you, and you've been spending a lot of money
lately. Money that should have gone to him!"

"Don't be ridiculous," Uncle J replied. "I
haven't spent a thing. I haven't had the time."

The first one pushed the knife closer. I could see a tiny drop of blood on the blade.

"Recognize the knife, Iscariot?" he sneered. "We took it as partial payment the last time you owed us money."

Uncle J forced a smile. "Well, you've kept it sharp. I'll give you credit for that."

"Credit?" the knife-man laughed. "That's the problem, isn't it, Iscariot? You. And credit." Then he turned to the other man, the man with his hand around my neck. "Go on, tell him," he ordered. "Tell him what we've seen him buying on our boss's credit!"

"First day of the week," big-hand-man grunted. "You rented a donkey and its colt – just outside the city.

"Second day of the week, you paid a huge amount of money to the Temple authorities for wrecked tables and escaped doves.

"Third day of the week, you put a deposit on

a first floor room…"

"Wait! Wait!" my uncle interrupted. "None of those were my own expenses. Jesus wanted to enter the city on a donkey. He busted up a few things in the Temple. And he needs a room for the Passover. All of those expenses were for him!"

"His boss," I added. Though, with the man's hand around my throat, it came out kind of croaky.

"He's not my boss!" Uncle J sighed. "How many times do I have to tell you that?"

"But he lets you spend his money?" asked knife-man.

"It's all our money. Sort of. People give it to us. Rich women. Other supporters. And Jesus… well… Jesus more or less put me in charge of it."

Big-hand-man loosened his grip a bit, threw back his head, and roared with laughter.

"He put YOU in charge of the money? YOU? I thought this Jesus was some kind of prophet. He's gotta know better than that!"

"I don't know what he knows," Uncle J muttered. "But he is a second-chance kind of person, so maybe…"

"Maybe he still trusts you?" chuckled knife-man. "And you're telling us that you have never, shall we say, 'borrowed' from this fund of his?"

I looked at Uncle J. He looked at the ground.

"Yeah, well, maybe once or twice," he mumbled. "But I can't do it again! I mean it. There's this other disciple, John. He's always watching now. I think he's on to me."

"Not our problem," knife-man replied. "But it is your problem. And if you don't come up with the goods by the first day of next week, this knife of yours is going to find its way back to its owner, in a not-very-pleasant manner. Do I make myself clear?"

Uncle J nodded.
"Very clear."

"Then our business is done," said knife-man. "For the present, at least."

"Can I let go of the kid, now?" asked big-hand-man. "My fingers are cramping."

So the knife-man put his knife away. The other took his big mitt off my throat.

And they walked away, down the street.

Uncle J stood there, silent. I rubbed my neck.

"So what are you going to do?" I asked, at last.

"I don't know! I don't know!" he shouted. "I thought I told you to go home!"

"Sorry," I said. "I'm just trying to help."

"Well, you can't help, all right!" he was still shouting. And then he hung his head and sighed. "Unless, of course, you've got twenty-nine pieces of silver on you."

"Whoa. That's a lot of money!" I replied.

"Worth killing a man for," he nodded. "I've seen people die for far less."

And then, suddenly, there were two more men standing behind Uncle J. But they were as different from the first men as two sets of people could be.

I looked up and coughed and gestured.

Uncle J leaped to his feet, fists clenched. "I told you I'd get your money!" he cried, turning around. But when he saw the men, he stepped back. He settled down. And he apologized.

"Sorry, I thought you were someone else."

"Apparently," one of the men smiled. "No harm done."

The other man looked at me. He was smiling, too.

"We're priests, young man. And we wondered if we could have a word with your friend?"

"Ahhh, more religious people," I thought. "Not nearly as interesting as the guys with the knives and big hands, but not nearly as dangerous, either."

That's what I thought. But all I said was, "He's my uncle, actually." And I smiled back.

"With your uncle, then," said the first priest. "It won't take long. We couldn't help but overhear and think we might have a way to help him with his problem."

Uncle J shrugged, gave me a puzzled look, and walked off with them. And in no time at all, he was back.

"So did it work?" I asked. "Are they gonna give you the money?"

"Yeah," he nodded, quietly.

"Amazing!" I shouted. "That's amazing!" And then I paused. "They don't want you to kill anybody or anything, do they?"

"Don't be ridiculous," he grunted. "I don't do that any more. You know that. No, they just want me to do them a favour. Introduce them to somebody. That's all. It should be fine."

"Introduce them to somebody? For twenty-nine pieces of silver?" I laughed. "That must be some special guy!"

"Yeah," he nodded again, more quietly still. "He is. And it's thirty pieces of silver, actually. I hope I've made the right choice."

"Are you kidding?" I said. "What a deal! You are the coolest guy ever, Uncle J. Spy. Rabbi. Wheeler-dealer. I want to be just like you when I grow up."

"Thanks kid," he muttered, as he turned to walk away. But maybe you'd be better off…" And then he stopped, mid-sentence.

"Never mind," he finished, as he waved goodbye. "See you around, kid."

And I waved back. "See you around, Uncle J."

The Neighbour's Version

Jesus is Put to Death on the Cross

I always looked up to my next-door neighbour, Aaron.

He was older than me, by ten years. But if any of the other kids started bullying me, he would always be there, to tell them off or fight them off or whatever.

I remember this time when Daniel, up the street, was chasing me. I don't even remember why, but he was bigger than me and it happened a lot. I was almost home, almost safe, when I tripped and fell face first in the dirt.

And just as he was about to jump on me and pound me, Aaron showed up, grabbed him by the collar, and hoisted him in the air.

"You want to mess with my neighbour?" he growled. "You'll have to mess with me first."

Then he dropped Daniel, who took off at once and didn't stop running until he'd reached the end of the street.

Aaron grinned and helped me up, and his mum asked me in and gave me a piece of a cake she'd been making. Then Aaron went off to work with a "You tell me if he gives you any more trouble" and another grin.

I always looked up to Aaron. So when my mum told me that he'd been arrested, it was a big shock.

"What do you mean?" I asked. "What did he do? They must have the wrong guy!"

But all she could do was cry and shake her head. And then, when she stopped crying, she said, "He stole. Stole from his boss. And you know what that means."

I did.

Aaron worked for a tax collector. He didn't actually collect the taxes. And he definitely wasn't one of those guys who went around breaking people's arms if they didn't pay. He did the accounts. That's all. He kept the books.

But because stealing from tax collectors was pretty much the same as stealing from the Roman government, he was in really big trouble.

"That's just what they say, though, isn't it?" I asked my mum. "He didn't really do it, did he?"

She shook her head again. "Who knows? But if they arrested him, they must be pretty certain."

I pounded a fist into the palm of my hand. "I bet it was a set-up. I bet it was that tax collector he works for. He even *looks* evil."

"It doesn't matter," my mum shrugged. "The Romans will use this as an example to keep other people from stealing."

"But that's not fair!" I shouted. "Not if he didn't do it!"

"Life's not fair," she sighed. "It's not fair that the Romans occupy our country. It's not fair that our taxes pay for them to do it. It's not fair that their soldiers seize ordinary people and put them to work for nothing." And here her voice got really quiet. "And it's not fair that some of those people die in terrible accidents."

She was talking about my dad. Lots of conversations finished with him. And I can see why. If the soldiers hadn't grabbed him and forced him to load their supply wagon, then

he wouldn't have been there, at the back, when the brakes let go and the wagon started rolling. And the wagon wouldn't have run him over.

Six years ago – that's when it happened. I was only five. And maybe that's why I always think of sadness when I think about my mum. And maybe that's why I looked up to Aaron.

He was always there for me, like the big brother I never had. And he was never sad. Ever.

People say that accountants are boring. Not Aaron. He cracked jokes and did these stupid magic tricks and was always bringing me surprises. It's like he was making up for my dad not being there. And he did a really good job of it.

And that's why it was even more shocking, a few days later, when my mum told me that the judge had found him guilty.

"I don't believe it!" I said. "They must have got something wrong."

Sadly, she shook her head. "No. I talked to his mum. Turns out that Aaron likes a bit of a flutter. He stole the money to pay off his gambling debts."

"So how long will he have to stay in prison?" I asked. And that's when the tears started again.

"Not long," she wept. "He's due to be executed. Tomorrow."

"For stealing?" I cried. "That's not fair!"

"How many times do I have to tell you?" she sighed. "Life's not fair."

"I want to see him, then!" I pleaded. "Just one more time."

"A crucifixion is no place for a child," she said. And she said it like she really meant it.

But I didn't feel like a child. Never have really. So I was going. I didn't care what she said.

Crucifixions in Jerusalem are always on the top of this hill they call 'The Skull'. It fits, I guess. Skulls and executions.

So that's where I headed, early next morning,

once my mum had gone. I thought I'd have to be careful – so she wouldn't see me. But, for some reason, the streets were packed. So I just mingled in with the crowd.

It was strange, really strange. Some people were laughing. Some were shouting. Others were crying like they'd lost their best friend.

"What's going on?" I said to a man as he pushed past me.

"Where have you been, boy?" the man grunted. "They tried Rabbi Jesus last night. Found him guilty, too."

"Guilty of what?" I asked.

"Blasphemy," grunted another man. "Apparently all those miracles have gone to his head. He says he's God. He says he wants to tear down the Temple."

"That's what they SAY he said!" a woman shouted angrily. "I don't believe a word of it. He healed my little girl. He was the nicest man I ever met!"

"They don't crucify Nice People," the man grunted back.

And I couldn't help thinking about Aaron. Okay, maybe he did steal from that tax collector. But he was always nice to me.

The crowd pushed and shoved its way up the hill. I couldn't see my mum. I couldn't see Aaron, either. But I saw someone else.

"Jesus!" some lady cried.

"Jesus!" spat some man.

And there he was – staggering up the hill, a wooden cross beam on his ripped-up back, a ring of thorns digging into his head. And there was blood; blood everywhere. I felt like I was going to be sick.

Then he stumbled. And he fell. And the soldiers grabbed this man out of the crowd and made him carry the cross beam instead.

When we got to the top of The Skull, they

nailed the beam to another one, to make the
shape of a cross. And then – I couldn't believe it
– they nailed Jesus to the wood, as well!

The nails went through his wrists and his
ankles, and there was even more blood. And I
couldn't help thinking, were they doing this to
Aaron, too, somewhere else on this hill?

"It's not fair!" someone shouted. "He doesn't
deserve this."

And he didn't. No one did. Not to be treated

like that. My mum was right. Life's not fair.

And that's when she spotted me.

"What are you doing here?" she shouted. "I told you to stay home!"

"But I had to come! I had to!" I replied. "I have to say goodbye to Aaron."

She fell to her knees then and folded herself into a ball and just cried and cried. I didn't know what to say. So I sort of crouched down beside her and put my arms around her neck.

"I'm sorry, Mum," I whispered. "I just want to see him. Please."

She stopped sobbing, at last, and wiped her eyes and pointed. "He's over there."

I walked slowly, really slowly, toward his cross. And the closer I got, the less sure I was that I wanted to be there. And then, there I was.

I'd always looked up to Aaron. And, sadly, I was looking up, now, as well.

His cross was standing next to Jesus'. But he hadn't been nailed like the rabbi – only tied to the beam. That was a relief. And there wasn't even much blood. Just bruises, mostly. But he was having trouble breathing. It was like he had to pull himself up to take a breath – and it looked like that was a really, really hard thing for him to do.

I didn't say anything. I didn't know what to

say. And when his eyes caught mine, I wondered if I'd done the right thing coming after all. He looked so hurt and embarrassed.

"I'm… sorry," he struggled to say. "I'm… so… sorry."

And that's when I started to cry.

I wanted to be brave. I really did. But to see him there – Aaron, who'd been like a brother to me – and to know that I'd never see him again and always have to remember him like this. It was too much.

His mum put her arm around me. She was crying, too. My mum joined us. And we all just stood there – sad and pathetic and hopeless.

And then somebody started shouting.

"Jesus! Jesus!" came a voice from the cross on the other side of the rabbi. "You saved blind people. Deaf people. Lame people. Why don't you save yourself – and us with you?"

I looked at the man. His eyes were puffy and swollen and bruised. But I still recognized his evil face.

"That's the tax collector!" I said. "The one Aaron works for. But I thought…"

"They were in it together," Aaron's mum sighed. "They were both stealing – from the Romans."

And then Aaron spoke. It took him a while to find the breath. He pulled himself up slowly and he croaked back.

"Leave the rabbi alone. You and me – we deserve to be here. But he's done nothing wrong."

And then he looked at Jesus – looked him right in the eye – and said, "Remember me, please, when you get to someplace better."

And Jesus? Jesus looked right back at him and said, "Today. Today you will be with me – in Paradise."

And that's when Aaron smiled. Smiled like the times he'd told his favourite joke. Smiled like the times he'd played a trick on someone. Smiled like the times he'd showed up at the door with a surprise for me.

And I looked up at him and smiled back. And

he winked. And he shut his eyes. And my mum took my hand and led me away. And I went with her gladly. And that's the last I saw of him.

It's been a couple of months now since Aaron died. And Jerusalem has not stopped buzzing.

Not because of him. Or his boss. But because of Jesus.

They say he came back to life.

They say his friends saw him and talked to him and ate with him.

They say that he took them up a hill and that he just rose straight up into heaven.

I don't know what I think about any of that. But I hope it's true. Because if Jesus is in heaven, then Aaron is, too.

Life may not be fair. People still don't get what they deserve. But if that means, in Paradise, thieves get forgiveness instead of the punishment they deserve, then that's probably a good thing.

Must remember to mention that to Mum.

The Yawner's Version

Paul Performs a Miracle

"Mum," I said. "I'm tired. I've been working all day!"

"Mum," I said. "I don't like 'lectures' at the best of times. Give me something to do, yes, and I'm with you. But to just sit there and listen to some guy talking. It's not really my thing."

"Mum," I said. "I'm glad that this Jesus stuff you're into makes you happy. Everybody needs a hobby. I'm pleased that you found yours. But a guy coming back from the dead? That's a step or three too far for me. So you go. And don't worry. I'll make myself some dinner."

I tried every excuse in the book. I really did. But your mum is your mum. And when she gives you that look like you're killing her because you won't do what she wants you to do, it's hard to say "no".

And that's how I found myself on the third floor of some meeting hall in the middle of Troas. Sitting on a windowsill. As far back and as far away from the speaker as I could get.

Mum was up front. Of course! With a bunch of her friends, yapping and gabbing like she hadn't seen them for months. Except she sees them every week. And sometimes in the middle of the week, too. They keep her busy. And that's a good thing, I guess.

Like I said, they were yapping, but when the lecture started, they shut right up, and leaned forward, like it was some god or some hero that was talking.

Their fascination with the guy escaped me at first. He was a bit of a runt, to be honest, with a lazy eye and a tendency to talk without taking a breath. But he seemed sincere enough, like he really believed in what he was saying. I'd go so far as to say that he was passionate about it – and obviously wanted the rest of us to be passionate, too.

He started with the same story I'd heard from my mum. About this Jewish teacher called Jesus, who lived in Judea back when Tiberius was the emperor. He was supposed to be some long-awaited saviour of the Jews. He taught people about God. He did miracles. But then he upset some of the leaders and he was put to death. End of story.

Except that this Paul, who was speaking, said that wasn't actually the end of the story. He said that this Jesus didn't stay dead – that he came back to life after three days, and then went up into heaven. As I say, more than a bit of a stretch from my point of view.

But then he said something that really did get my attention. He said that he had actually seen this Jesus, after he came back from the dead! He had been an enemy of Jesus' followers and was chasing them and arresting them, and was on this trip to Damascus, when Jesus appeared to him in a vision or something and talked to him. And after that, he became a follower of Jesus, himself, and travelled around the world, telling people about him.

I made a mental note to try and talk to him about that when he was done speaking. Did he really see this Jesus, or was it some kind of hallucination thing – just his imagination?

There was supposed to be some kind of meal afterwards, so I thought there might be a chance to get him off to one side.

The problem was, once he'd finished with the story bit, he just kept talking. And I have to say, it wasn't as interesting. My mum looked like she was still listening. She was leaning forward and all. But she'd been part of this group for a little while and understood more of what was going on. And she hadn't been working all day.

I, on the other hand, had been up with the sun, and had been down loading and unloading boats at the dock. My uncle – my mum's brother – got me the job. And even though it was hard, it kept us going, which we needed, since my dad was dead.

I thought about other stuff at first. About the job. About going fishing. About what we were having for dinner. I was starving!

But the guy just kept talking!

I thought about sneaking out, but every ten minutes or so, my mum would look back at me and smile. No chance to escape, then.

Then I looked out the window. It was a long way down, but I could pick out the people walking past – what they were wearing, what they were doing. I started to count them, but that was probably the worst thing I could have done. Okay, they weren't sheep, but they might as well have been. Because the more I counted, the sleepier I got.

It was just a yawn or two at first, but then I

couldn't stop doing it.
So I watched the
speaker guy again,
but I had no idea
what he was talking
about by this time.

Mum smiled
again.
I smiled back. And
then my eyes snapped
shut. I was asleep, but
just for a second. Or
that's what
it felt like. What time was it?

And then, you know how it is – the harder
you try to stay awake, the
harder it is to actually
do it. The eyes kept
closing, the guy's voice
kept fading. And then
I'd force myself awake
again. And then the
whole thing would
repeat itself.

I pinched my leg a couple of times, I shifted my bottom, I did everything I could think of. And then I thought, what did it matter? If my mum asked me what I thought, I could always say I liked the first part and leave it at that. I didn't need to stay awake. So I gave in. I fell asleep.

And that's when I started to dream. Nice dreams at first. I was out on the boat with my uncle. I was fishing. It was hot and sunny. The water was reflecting off the sea. Then I was eating. Better still. This lamb roast my mum makes. Delicious.

But then, someone was chasing me. Don't know who. I was running. I was trying to get away. So I climbed up these steps. Up and up and up. I was on a roof. He was after me. Couldn't see his face. It was dark. I was scared. I ran to the edge of the roof. I tripped. And like happens in dreams all the time, I started to fall.

They say that if you fall in a dream and hit the ground and die, that you die in real life. Which I always thought was ridiculous. But that doesn't stop you from not wanting to hit the ground in your dream. So I did what everybody does when they're falling in their dream. I forced myself awake. And, much to my surprise, what I discovered was that I

actually was falling! The ground was rushing toward me, but there was no waking up this time. Only darkness, as my head hit the street below.

And that should have been it. End of story. But then I heard my name.

"Eutychus."

Off in the distance. But my name, nonetheless.

And when I had forced one eye open, like waking from a dream, there was another eye peering into it. A lazy eye.

And then somebody said, "He's alive!" And somebody cheered and somebody cried and several somebodies picked me up and carried me back up into the room. Somebody grabbed my hand, too. But I knew who that was. No need for guessing there.

"Sorry, Mum," I whispered. "I fell asleep. I fell out the window. I thought I was going to die."

"What do you mean, 'thought'?" said one of the men who was carrying me. "You did die, boy! And Paul brought you back to life again!"

"Hush!" said my mum. "There's no need to go into it – not yet. Let him get his strength back first!"

"But it's a miracle!" said one of the other men. "Everybody ought to know!"

"All in good time," said my mum. And she squeezed my hand again. "I'm just so glad that you're all right," she sniffled.

"Me, too," I groaned. "Me, too."

So they laid me down upstairs and everybody had this meal that they call the eucharist, which means "thanks", which seemed particularly appropriate that night, especially for me and my mum.

I never did get to talk to that Paul about him seeing Jesus. I thanked him, of course – more thanks – but it didn't seem right, somehow, to question whether he'd talked to a man who'd come back from the dead – seeing as he'd sort of helped me do that, too.

And that's my little tale, I guess.

I listened to a talk by a man called Paul. It went on a bit long. I fell asleep. I fell three storeys out of a window. End of story.

Not!